From
John & Marcia
May – 2002

From
John & Marcia
May – 2002

SENSATIONAL BOUQUETS

BY *Christian Tortu*

ARRANGEMENTS BY A MASTER FLORAL DESIGNER

SENSATIONAL BOUQUETS

BY *Christian Tortu*

ARRANGEMENTS BY A MASTER FLORAL DESIGNER

PHOTOGRAPHS BY SYLVAIN THOMAS

with text by Corine Delahaye
Preface by Christian Tortu

Harry N. Abrams, Inc., Publishers

Project Manager, English-language edition: Ellen Nidy
Editor, English-language edition: Matthew Giles
Design Coordinator, English-language edition: Tina Thompson

Library of Congress Cataloging-in-Publication Data

Delahaye, Corine.
Sensational bouquets by Christian Tortu : arrangements by a master
floral designer / by Corine Delahaye ; with photographs by Sylvain
Thomas ; preface by Christian Tortu.
    p. cm.
  ISBN 0-8109-5731-0
  1. Bouquets. I. Thomas, Sylvain. II. Title.
  SB449.5.B65 D46 2001
  745.92'2—dc21
                        00-066380

Copyright 2000 Éditions Minerva, Geneva
English translation © 2001 Harry N. Abrams, Inc.

Published in 2001 by Harry N. Abrams, Incorporated, New York

Printed and bound in France

Harry N. Abrams, Inc.
100 Fifth Avenue
New York, N.Y. 10011
www.abramsbooks.com

CONTENTS

PREFACE

All flowers are green buds before they open and reveal their brilliant colors. Their goal is to draw attention to themselves, if not immediately, then in time. By any means necessary, they have to become the fruit, which will carry the seed, which will yield the plant, which will continue the cycle of life in the world of flowers.

Green are the young shoots, a symbol of hope; green are the stems and leaves, the sepal and calyx. Flowers that are all grouped in the same chromatic family will only exude their ephemeral charm when it's time to be courted.

Their green bears the color of hope and freedom. Each plant is a fragment of a landscape, playing the same music found in all the harmony of time, and yet, man wants to class them by genus, family, and species; and it is this order that has influenced our apprehension of the plant world for ages. After two centuries, we are questioning the foundations of this classification. We now wonder whether a rose and a cabbage don't in fact belong to the same family. What a lesson!

If man were to stop rushing around for one moment, he might take a look at flowers—and then take a closer look. He would see all that is green and all that is around him. In time, his convictions would crumble, and he would realize that classification is fruitless even beyond flowers.

Christian Tortu

GENESIS

GENESIS

In the beginning there was nature. The whole story of Tortu, the man, the florist, and the designer, starts here, in the garden of his parents, truck farmers in France's Anjou region, during his walks with his grandfather, and on beaten paths and hidden trails.

It's no secret: Christian Tortu is proud of his peasant background. His family has been producing crops for the market for generations. The work is hard, but life is sweet, filled with the moments of happiness that nature provides. A few wild flowers grow against a wall; other greenery with highlights of many colors gather along the road, and are placed by his mother in clay pots near a window in the house.

Raised by the rhythms of the seasons, Tortu learned about nature on his daily treks across his native countryside with the horizon as his only limit. Unpretentious, unostentatious nature. He only had to look to understand. Every single one of his bouquets has drawn inspiration from here ever since: he reinterprets raw nature, depending on how he is feeling, what he is doing, and the colors of the season.

His creations start with wild grasses that grow between two cobblestones, with a graceful flowering apple tree branch from an orchard, or with a modest lettuce covered in dew. Although filled with harmony, Tortu's perspective is nevertheless subversive: his poetic tension makes light of manners and rules, nudges preconceived ideas, and takes us on a journey to a place without prejudice and boundaries.

In the beginning there was nature. The whole story of Tortu, the man, the florist, and the designer, starts here, in the garden of his parents, truck farmers in France's Anjou region, during his walks with his grandfather, and on beaten paths and hidden trails.

It's no secret: Christian Tortu is proud of his peasant background. His family has been producing crops for the market for generations. The work is hard, but life is sweet, filled with the moments of happiness that nature provides. A few wild flowers grow against a wall; other greenery with highlights of many colors gather along the road, and are placed by his mother in clay pots near a window in the house.

Raised by the rhythms of the seasons, Tortu learned about nature on his daily treks across his native countryside with the horizon as his only limit. Unpretentious, unostentatious nature. He only had to look to understand. Every single one of his bouquets has drawn inspiration from here ever since: he reinterprets raw nature, depending on how he is feeling, what he is doing, and the colors of the season.

His creations start with wild grasses that grow between two cobblestones, with a graceful flowering apple tree branch from an orchard, or with a modest lettuce covered in dew. Although filled with harmony, Tortu's perspective is nevertheless subversive: his poetic tension makes light of manners and rules, nudges preconceived ideas, and takes us on a journey to a place without prejudice and boundaries.

All flowers are created equal

In my home, when I was growing up, my family had traditional flowers from the florist, and then other ones that we would find around our home and in the countryside. In other words, not much! There were the chosen ones, the "beautiful" flowers with their aura of prestige, upright, straight, proud, all held together in cellophane. Then, there was the immense diversity of the plant kingdom, but it was never displayed or offered as a gift. Perhaps we never even wanted to see it. And yet, how could we have said that a flower, a fruited branch, or some foliage wasn't worthy of a bouquet? Who forbade it? And why?

Nature is a good guide; it teaches us everything. All we have to do is let ourselves be taken down paths that cross our land and look. Everywhere, at all times, it generously offers us color, form, and scent: flowers, fruits, vegetables, branches, and foliage are intertwined, mixed together lawlessly, without artifice or ostentation. Variations are linked together by the play of sunlight and the help of clouds. Nature is a place of total freedom. Here, all plant life is accepted as equal, because nature doesn't label with a price tag. Everything is worth the same amount. No matter the shape, color,

or condition, all forms of plant life are simply there, living in harmony. The door to all possibilities can therefore be opened. Multiple combinations form a bountiful palette of textures, hues, scents, and feelings.

Nature fosters all languages. It is a place of unlimited creation constantly being renewed. The bouquet is one of nature's forms of writing, but the language stays the same: a language of freedom and equality. One should not deprive oneself of anything. All plant life deserves to be mentioned, even the least noble, the most obscure, the most ephemeral. Leaving pomposity behind, we are left with the power of controlled chaos, rearranged to communicate the beauty of a landscape.

All plant life is born free and equal. It is in the name of this "declaration of the rights of plant life" that Christian Tortu arranges his bouquets. Nature is his model, and just like nature, he does not exclude or isolate. His only limits are those presented by nature itself, which is forever changing from one season to the next.

When species intermingle, a bouquet takes shape
and fills with life. A priori, cultivated thistles
would never find themselves beside wild thistles,
which are rougher, tormented, and more
modest in color. And yet, the star structure of
other thistles has only to take over: together,
they weave a tender green spider's web in which
other bred thistles, with bluish stems and
deep purple petals, can be inserted.
Their union is miraculously soft. Harmony is
expressed in a bouquet of rounded shapes . . .
and full of prickles!

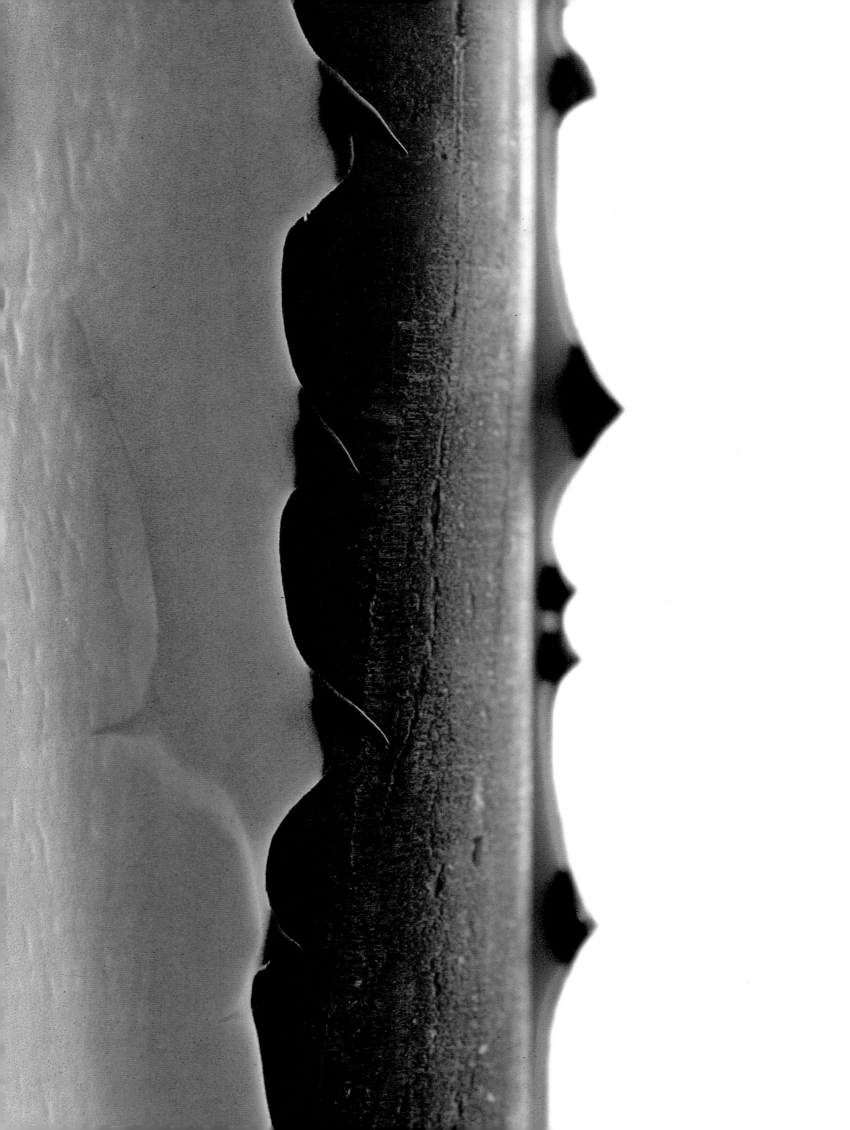

Nature proposes, the eye disposes.
We need only to know how to look at the plant world,
how to respect the uniqueness of species, and to accept
their natural tendencies. We mustn't force them,
but reveal them. We mustn't change their nature,
spruce them up. Above all, we must awaken them.

A rose's authenticity is rediscovered. Considered a "noble" species,
roses are, for the most part, mistreated. They are arranged
to stand rigidly and alone in their crystal vase, as if they were
to be glorified and never "compromised" by the presence of
other species. As orphans, they seem bored. Yet, like all flowers,
roses have a story. They belong to a family, a garden.
They live in a community, with other flowers, fruit, and trees.
This is how they exist in all their intensity and also in all their fragility:
next to a stone wall, within the depths of an orchard, slightly hidden,
secret, and yet there to be viewed by an attentive eye.

The flower in all its stages -

A flower is not only beautiful when we call it beautiful. Almost all plant life goes through a flower stage. But flowering is always just an ephemeral stage in the overall life of the plant. A simple stem, and then a bud, it blooms and wilts before becoming a seed again. The plant's life cycle is Christian Tortu's frame of reference: he loves flowers in all their stages. For flowers tell of a universal life, a life during which decomposition is inevitable, a life of never more, a life of constant rebirth and exceeded limits. Today's wilted flower is the seed for tomorrow's tree, a tree that will outlive us and whose roots will bring down our walls. The life of a plant challenges the cornerstones of a civil society where space seems too regulated, too narrow, too simplified. All plant life, whether above ground or below, is movement. It never sleeps, and its cycle is never broken. The seasons come one after the other tirelessly and stubbornly, but not without hazards and conflicts. With a late frost, the hope for early fruit harvest deflates, and yet, life is born again, now and forever.

To say that a flower is beautiful when it is in full bloom is obvious. It's a common remark and, at the same time, inevitable: in fact, a flower

fulfills its destiny. When a flower shows its beauty, it is flirting. It above all wants to make itself desirable so that it can seduce the insect that will pollinate it, and it has no time to lose. It puts on its best, and dresses in many colors to attract attention. It puts on perfume. It opens, offers itself, gives itself over.

The flower's efforts pay off in this period of splendor. It is courted, admired, and celebrated in all respects. The flower is honored and placed on a pedestal. Its fall is all the more brutal.

Soon, the flower withers. Petals droop and fall one by one. Soon it seems that the flower can only inspire melancholy and sadness. It is asked to leave the premises, disappear. As if it had nothing left to show or prove, having lost its perfect shape, its color, its youth. As if it no longer deserved to exist. As if no one could see what the flower was hiding, what it was trying to say. As if age were meant to be a period of solitude and neglect. As if the flower were bluntly reminding man of his own destiny to recount how difficult it is to know how to live in fleeting time.

A flower wilts, a life begins.
A flower can also be beautiful once it loses its petals.
It's beautiful because it's without pomp and artifice.
It is beautiful because it doesn't suggest an end
of a life, but the beginning of another one . . .
beauty is a matter of seeing.

As ephemeral as they are, flowers bear a form of eternity.
Plant life is always a new beginning.
Each flower is a moment in this story;
every stage of the flower is a moment in life
that deserves attention.

Green all over

Entirely green bouquets: what better homage can be paid to nature? Or must there be the premise of a subversive approach?

An entirely green bouquet is surely a variation on the theme of all plants being created equal. But, for Tortu, green all over is the echo of an aesthetic emotion rooted in his childhood: a time when he would bring back a branch he found on the side of the path with his grandfather and place it somewhere in the house. Playing grownup!

Nothing should be excluded a priori. We must take all that nature makes available to us. Henceforth, foliage is not only used in a bouquet to accompany flowers and to enhance them; it is a bouquet in itself. It climbs up the sides of pots, displaying all the nuance of green and offering a gulp of nature every time. Nothing but foliage . . . is this another way of plunging into the green?

Green is the color of renewal and hope, a metaphor for freshness in the collective imagination. Green symbolizes many things in different cultures, but, in our part of the world, green is the primary color of the landscape. It is the color that almost magically appears when nature emerges out of its gray and brown winter to come alive again

and present an infinite palette of greens. It eventually obscures other colors with its dominance. One has to get close to discover berries within a bush, flowers in the undergrowth and out in the field, and fruit in the trees. Foliage plays hide-and-go-seek and sometimes proves to be capricious when springtime is late. Dark or light, vivid or soft, emerald or translucent, it upsets the balance and comes to life. The bearer of all symbolic riches, green punctuates Tortu's creations: his bouquets, of course, but also his perfumes, his lotions, and the candles he designs. The symbol of nature par excellence, foliage irrigates Tortu's entire creative process.

Foliage is inconceivable in the singular.
It is plural: not just for the intensity and range
of colors it presents, but also for the variety
of its slender or stout forms, its density,
and the thickness and shape of the leaves themselves.
Green creates itself, structures itself.
Green becomes matter. Full of a vital, almost raw, force,
it coats, embraces, piles itself up and then, subtly, veils
and unveils, delicately revealing another dash of color.

64

Green: a color, a thin slice from the light spectrum,
becomes a principle of life for a whole part of nature.
The most secret alchemy of a living organism
comes to the fore, saturating our eyes.

REVOLUTION(S)

REVOLUTION(S)

A florist who begins his career with a profession of faith in the form of a "declaration of the rights of plant life," and who asserts that all plant life is created equal, clearly holds the seed of revolution within. Therefore, in order to help his fellow man understand the world's beauty, Christian Tortu does not shy away from challenging our habits, from breaking the rules with steadfast determination, but with great gentleness. Over the years, something has been stirring inside. He has set sail for the city, leaving the country behind. He has gone from nature to culture, but nature has remained present, intact, and impossible to forget. Nature has entered the city with all of its vigor, confident about its power. Down with superficial ornamentation, tools and props, and

the accumulation of mostly barbarous superfluity! Ring in the reign of the raw, organic power of plant life! The goal is clear: to refresh the imagination, to abolish purely decorative presumptions, and to not copy the picturesque aspect of forms. One must create forms from the thing itself, to always be inspired by nature which, in spite of its diversity, is both resolute and economical with its motifs.

Tortu's boutique in Paris is a nature reserve in the heart of the Latin Quarter. He doesn't offer bouquets, only the art of living, which begins with the art of seeing: flowers are no longer knickknacks, unchanging objects, but rather living elements that can make life softer and more beautiful.

A florist who begins his career with a profession of faith in the form of a "declaration of the rights of plant life,", and who asserts that all plant life is created equal, clearly holds the seed of revolution within. There-fore, in order to help his fellow man understand the world's beauty, Christian Tortu does not shy away from challenging our habits, from breaking the rules with steadfast determination, but with great gen-tleness. Over the years, something has been stirring inside. He has set sail for the city, leaving the country behind. He has gone from nature to culture, but nature has remained present, intact, and impossible to forget. Nature has entered the city with all of its vigor, confident about its power. Down with superficial ornamentation, tools and props, and

the accumulation of mostly barbarous superfluity! Ring in the reign of the raw, organic power of plant life! The goal is clear: to refresh the imagination, to abolish purely decorative presumptions, and to not copy the picturesque aspect of forms. One must create forms from the thing itself, to always be inspired by nature which, in spite of its diver-sity, is both resolute and economical with its motifs.

Tortu's boutique in Paris is a nature reserve in the heart of the Latin Quarter. He doesn't offer bouquets, only the art of living, which begins with the art of seeing: flowers are no longer knickknacks, unchanging objects, but rather living elements that can make life softer and more beautiful.

The color revolution

In the years Tortu spent in the country, he learned about nature by rubbing shoulders with it. It was a nature that only asked for aesthetic contemplation in order to teach about beauty and tolerance, authenticity, and openness to all possibilities. Tortu applied its lessons from the beginning, first at his boutique right near the Odéon in Paris, and then on Rue des Quatre-Vents.

He began surreptitiously by playing with chromatic ranges of colors, bending the rules of tradition and good taste. He rediscovered forgotten colors, colors once considered improper for a bouquet arrangement. He dared to put together unseemly combinations so that we could feel the emotion of a wild garden or a winding path. At the same time, the city challenged some of his country convictions: by being in the city, in the throng of variety and constant activity, Tortu discovered new combinations and new chromatic palettes. Sometimes the urban colors were inherently different—more artificial, more chemical—and sometimes they blended in new ways, depending on the wanderings of the city's inhabitants. As if all city flowers were the men, women, and children strolling the streets, even

the iridescent, amazingly shiny colors of the cars. As if city dwellers were to the city what flowers were to the field.

Tortu's love of color also led him to indulge in monochromatic arrangements. He took the idea a step further, however, by creating bouquets in matching tones, but in traditionally unworthy hues: beiges, whites, grays, and blacks. Nothing was excluded, not even the colors of the city.

The door to inspiration is open to entirely white, green, red, and blue bouquets, because full ranges of each color exist. Everything plays on the subtlety of half-tones and highlights, as if to stimulate our senses that were made dull by the absence of nature in urban life. New colors are brought out when new forms such as fruits and vegetables are introduced in a bouquet. Tortu is inspired by the soft green of lettuce, the deep purple of an eggplant, the cream granule of cabbage—which is nevertheless considered a flower—the dark brown of seeds, the amber-green of a pear. Color is not the only element of a bouquet. Texture also plays a role, introducing other subtleties: a velvet quality, a translucent quality, or a prickly or rough quality.

Harmony is built on surprising contrasts,
such as the diaphanous hue of a flower
that is being protected by some thick foliage
that seems to fall between animal and plant.

The form revolution

For a long time, in our homes, there were both flowers from the florist and those from outside, as we have said in previous pages. On one hand, ostentatious bouquets, dressed up and ready to go; and on the other hand, amateur bouquets, made of flowers and grasses freshly picked on a stroll through the countryside, bouquets arranged without preconceived notions, and which only reminded us of a moment.

A shapeless bouquet? A twisted bouquet? Which is which? Moreover, which one is really beautiful? A ceremonial bouquet, made purely for display, slightly arrogant, and meant only to reflect the social status of its buyer—the idea is a bit ridiculous, no? Round bouquets have emerged, less demonstrative and less official, but filled with nuance and a certain easygoing quality. For Tortu, the round bouquet is a way of taking the opposite view to a spray of flowers. The modesty of the former comes up against the arrogance of the latter, affected and rigid to the point that we worry about removing it from the paper in which it is wrapped. Stripped of its finery, the spray is most often transformed into a grotesque feather duster and placed in a vase—a painful experience that reaps few aesthetic rewards.

Smaller in size, the round bouquet fits into many containers: pots, pails, soup tureens, salad bowls. Once the tie has been unfastened, the bouquet unfurls and divides into two or three smaller ones that can each be placed around the house to echo one another. Being less formal, round bouquets are therefore suitable for today's tastes and lifestyles. It's no coincidence if the form revolution has led to another one: a vase revolution, in which function reigns over the value of what the vase is made. The clay vase, the glass vase, and even the plastic vase are gradually replacing the patrimonial crystal vases from wedding registries of yesteryear.

But let there be no mistake. For Tortu, the round bouquet is neither an end in itself nor a model of symmetric geometry. To create a bouquet—round or other—is above all to create a shape within a shape, to use peaks and valleys, and also to play with time: as they bloom, flowers change in volume as much as in color and scent. The bouquet evolves and there is always something to discover; new architectural shapes are always being offered.

Plant life is the raw material with which the artist works in bulk; he sculpts it and makes adjustments according to place, vase, and person.

For Tortu, a bouquet's value has nothing to do with size or form.
Finally, extreme simplicity is the peak of sophistication.
Whether round, square, angled, or spindly, the bouquet
has to reveal emotion, balance, and grace.
If it doesn't, it is nothing. Without a soul, it doesn't exist.

The revolution in use

Tortu's bouquets like neither law nor order: in the name of harmony, each one has its own touch of anarchy. Behind each bouquet, there is a revolution!

Gradually, Tortu's style has developed into an art of divergence in which bouquets adopt unexpected colors and depart from typical forms. Even other plant life has been used, but nontraditionally. Fruits, vegetables, and herbs—always appreciated for their taste, texture, and scent—are also meant to be seen.

The bouquet burgeons into another dimension, disregarding rankings, boutique codes, and social standards. It becomes a synonym for well being, providing a simple way to respond to the new, but pressing need to have a bit of nature at home, for yourself; something to make you happy right there, in the kitchen or at the corner of your desk. It also becomes a means of communication and a way of sharing: the bouquet is no longer chosen for what it's worth or for what it could say about the person offering it, but rather for how it fits the personality of the person to whom it is being given: his or her tastes, lifestyle, or home. A bouquet can even echo a mix of styles in

a house—a unique bouquet for each individual. For each place, each room, there can be a specific bouquet: volumes, colors, and forms adapted to every desire.

The bouquet becomes the quintessence of sensation and emotion. It strives for pleasure and sometimes desire. It addresses someone and is no longer anonymous. It takes on a meaning, a personality. The social flower becomes one's own personal flower.

All stages of plant life are equally admirable. Painters and photographers have been proving this for ages: flowers, fruit, spikes, and seeds have filled Cézanne's, Chardin's, and Arcimboldo's canvases, and Karl Blossfeldt's photographs. The masterpieces of the genre were not all acknowledged in their time, even if they are referred to today.

And yet, it was a long time before floral art took chances. First there was the noble flower with its composed arrangements and clear motifs. For aesthetic reasons? In the name of savoir-faire? But, really, whose savoir-faire!

A bouquet is like a reflection of the soul. It takes shape
through a natural act. It announces the weather,
reflects the mood of the moment, and expresses joy
and sorrow. But the same bouquet will never be made
from the same flowers. It all depends on the hour,
moment, place, and time. A bouquet can do without motifs.
It needs nothing more than what it already has.

CROSSROADS

CROSSROADS

Christian Tortu's bouquets remind us that all things from nature are born of the same process of chance and necessity, a process that has been repeating itself for thousands of years. In this way, nature's creations are permanent and deny every possibility of an eternal established order.

The Surrealist poets, such as Max Ernst, wanted to create "an electric tension through the reciprocal maneuverings of elements that we have been accustomed to consider until now as odd and unrelated." Nature is very capable of this as well. First, it takes care of color and form, and then, function: it is, indeed, the work of a poet, to bring out the spark of the unexpected.

Tortu often says that he can only create if he is happy.

For to be happy is to be open: open to unknown factors and to unleashed intuition.

In this way, and every time he creates, Tortu reinvents these improbable hazards of nature, combining the rarest species with the simplest grasses, those "scented poor wretches" about which Colette spoke of so beautifully. He gives rise to an ephemeral world in which the most massive, the hardiest, and the most exotic, can coexist with the most fragile, the most humble, the most common, and the youngest seeds, flowers, fruits, vegetables, sprigs, branches, and rhizomes. Species, spaces, and generations are combined, and each bouquet praises democracy, like a hymn to tolerance. This intersection is Tortu's goal, a goal that is far from limited, and one that opens onto more combinations and other sources of inspiration to come.

Christian Tortu's bouquets remind us that all things from nature are born of the same process of chance and necessity, a process that has been repeating itself for thousands of years. In this way, nature's creations are permanent and deny every possibility of an eternal established order.

The Surrealist poets, such as Max Ernst, wanted to create "an electric tension through the reciprocal maneuverings of elements that we have been accustomed to consider until now as odd and unrelated." Nature is very capable of this as well. First, it takes care of color and form, and then, function: it is, indeed, the work of a poet, to bring out the spark of the unexpected.

Tortu often says that he can only create if he is happy.

For to be happy is to be open: open to unknown factors and to unleashed intuition.

In this way, and every time he creates, Tortu reinvents these improbable hazards of nature, combining the rarest species with the simplest grasses, those "scented poor wretches" about which Colette spoke of so beautifully. He gives rise to an ephemeral world in which the most massive, the hardiest, and the most exotic, can coexist with the most fragile, the most humble, the most common, and the youngest seeds, flowers, fruits, vegetables, sprigs, branches, and rhizomes. Species, spaces, and generations are combined, and each bouquet praises democracy, like a hymn to tolerance. This intersection is Tortu's goal, a goal that is far from limited, and one that opens onto more combinations and other sources of inspiration to come.

Integrating the exotic

Plant life invites us to go on a journey of the imagination. Images of nature speak to us of other places. Eventually we begin to dream of each one and have an irresistible need to go see, smell, and discover!

These are age-old temptations. The adventurers and explorers of yesteryear almost always wrote about finding new essences on their long journeys. These were chosen either for their medicinal or alimentary qualities, or simply for their beauty. This is how the first botanical gardens came about, small plots of land carefully labeled and numbered. Today we stroll up and down them just as we would flip through a travel journal.

Times have changed and exoticism is no longer the privilege of princes and scholars. In a flash, in a few hours on a plane, one can find plant life in its original habitat. Exotic plant life—be it flower, fruit, plant, or vegetable—has gradually become accessible, more familiar. The exotic is nearby, yet nevertheless retains a quality of the distant land where it has its roots. It has joined our world, bringing a host of scents, colors, and shapes that speak of other places and civilizations.

Christian Tortu will be remembered as one of the first to have used flowers from other lands in his floral designs. Not in the name of an exaggerated exoticism that could questionably involve traditional display, but simply as a way to communicate other emotions, to be open to other worlds with which we can coexist peacefully. It is a way of learning how to commingle with the different, how to live with the other.

A modest ambassador of a sometimes faraway nature, the bouquet therefore proves to have an ambitious mission: to be a quintessence of this "elsewhere" and, moreover, to be the center of all possibilities and of all plant or mineral species, from the most everyday and immediate to the most remote.

Tortu devises an intersection of the senses: for he is a florist who never forgets that working with flowers is one of the rare activities in which all the senses are called upon.

To go before what we have never seen, to strive to find the essential, to perceive, if not understand, one's private organization and one's emotional means. To become familiar with plant life by letting go of preconceived notions.

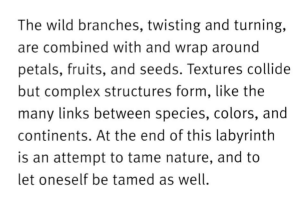

The wild branches, twisting and turning, are combined with and wrap around petals, fruits, and seeds. Textures collide but complex structures form, like the many links between species, colors, and continents. At the end of this labyrinth is an attempt to tame nature, and to let oneself be tamed as well.

Lessons from nature

Both an expression of life and of the ephemeral—a twofold paradoxical symbol of strength and fragility—a bouquet in its own way tells us about where we are, the weather outside, the mood of the moment, the instant of joy or sorrow. No need to draw on an arcane language of signs, not even on the very antique, but very social language of flowers—sélam—from Persia. By simply telling about nature, all natures, a bouquet secretly says that we are part and parcel. Nature is where learning takes place. Unpretentious and modest, it doesn't assert itself. Nature, very simply, is. But in all of its simplicity, it nevertheless proves to be complex and demanding, both with itself and with others. Nature is to be earned.

As in other areas, learning about nature only really happens when we come up against what is new and unusual, when we are exposed to another's difference and acceptance. Just as we must place plant life in its context, by putting it with everything that comes with it—stones, foliage, soil—we must bring in what is foreign, what is far away. Not to shock, but to find a full balance.

Authentic, like his sensibility, Tortu removes what is superfluous

in order to try to make his contribution to the happiness of others. He advances with his unusual arrangements, which are also lessons in modesty and tolerance. The happiness that comes from being in this world might be knowing how to integrate, to become one, to unify by taking an unhindered look at everything a priori. This is the first essential step.

Thus, we will be reasonable, we will ask for the impossible, and we will be demiurges. And yet, we are not overwhelmed by choice. We have a great feeling of freedom and autonomy, of complete balance.

Wherever he finds himself, Tortu never loses sight of his candid eye, in which a slightly skewed sense of humor is the weapon against all vanity. He creates as he sees: his strength lies in seeing differently and in knowing how to share his vision of the world.

To open oneself to the world and to make oneself happy.

To look at nature.

To stick to the original model.

To not deny oneself of anything.

To let an inner voice speak . . .

To silence one's mental state in order to allow one's senses to develop: this credo is also an asceticism . . . but, in truth, it is gentle.

The same flowers do not make the same bouquets.
Nothing is written in stone. It is by looking that
we learn. We think we're going to make a bouquet,
but, very soon after, it is the bouquet that is
making—or unmaking—us. Everyone can design
one's own bouquet, according to one's mood.
The secret is to open one's heart, to let go
of one's emotions, to keep going, to let oneself
be guided by nature and one's feeling and
to find room, room for oneself, here and now.

CHRONICLE OF A BLACK BOUQUET

July 1999: the Alpilles are on fire; a strong wind spreads the horror at a mind-blowing rate. An entire region is taken aback, and roads are blocked. It's impossible to know the size of the blaze, to know where the devastating wave has struck. Man is forced to acknowledge his impotence before such wild forces.

It is suspected that an arsonist's hand is the cause of the disaster. Outrage, disgust, and also shame because man is responsible for many forest fires every year. Does he need to burn a part of himself to this extent? Does he need to think for just one moment that he can dominate nature?

And so, while enduring the many hours of waiting behind the incredible wall of smoke and night, each and every person sees the landscapes that he or she took for granted, that he or she traveled so many times but never looked at enough, the landscapes that have so often been described, painted, captured by generations of souls marked by the spellbinding beauty of the area.

We have scheduled our first photographs for this book to be taken at this time. We of course feel the need to testify through a bouquet composed of plant life from the desolate area. We are not out to record final images of the site, for we know that the land will revive.

In the weeks and months following this apocalypse, the landscape was in mourning. Black predominated at all levels. The holiest of trees, hundred-year-old olive trees, were but pantomimes barely standing out against a background of gray, brown, and black. In some areas, the land and stones seemed to have attained such a great degree of incandescence that they were marked deep down in their flesh.

I painfully remember a herd of boars, adults and little ones, wandering aimlessly along the road, bewildered by what they had seen of hell. But were all the others—the unluckier ones—prisoners of the deadly trap? Nothing else seemed alive. For miles and miles, it looked like the end of the world.

A year later: the same roads, the same paths. Seen from afar, all is green again, a green that is unknown around here, almost worrisome. A uniform color, bordering on yellow. Vegetation has changed. As far as you can see, grasses weave a dense carpet covering the mountain, top to bottom. Getting closer, you can nevertheless see a range of subtle greens, made of thistles, holly, flowering scabrous.

For a second, one would think that nature had taken its place again. It's not true. Gone is the almost metallic green-gray of the olive trees, gone is the very particular green of the burgeoning vineyard, the darker green of the changing light hitting holm oak and pine trees. Only charred silhouettes haunt this lunar landscape. A few trees yielded some shoots that grow no higher than a young bush. We will never see the Alpilles that we knew again. Time is against us.

Once the olive and pine trees have been replanted, nature will have to begin its work again. To re-create the alchemy of the *garrigue* between broom, cysts, and dog rose. Giant reed will once again line paths. People will once again smell the familiar scent of rosemary, myrtle, and juniper. At that time, no one knows when, they will feel reassured by the omnipotence of nature, trusting its ability to forever reestablish what man has destroyed. But, we tend to forget that nature is fragile as well. We crave domination, and this surpasses all of our ancestral fears. And what if the sky fell on our heads?

Dead fish, naked trees, tides of many colors, deadly haze at the horizon. All of our indignation is in vain if we are not deeply conscious of our every act. Serious, often irreparable, whether it damages or builds, nature belongs to a time that outlives our own existence.

I would like to be optimistic, to be certain that I am not among the last to speak of this earth as it still stands, leaving generations to come only a taste of paradise lost.

Christian Tortu

THE BOUQUET ARRANGEMENTS

Squash flowers, foliage of scented leaf pelargoniums, and jasmine liana in a clay dish

Water lily flowers and leaves, water hyacinth and tea grass, in transparent vases and glasses (private collection)

Different varieties of thistles in a zinc bowl

Agave foliage and eucharis in gray wax vases

Guinea-hen flower, grape hyacinth, and Japanese maple in a silver tumbler

Tulips, phalaenopsis, and snowdrops in an Alvar Aalto vase

Crown imperial lily, cherry branches, and double tulips in a glass vase (Conran Shop)

Fruiting apple and pear tree branches, lavender

Garden roses, raspberry bush foliage, and mulberry in fig tree leaves

Pomegranate, African eggplant, and fruits de malus and solanum mamosum in an African clay vase

Green tomatoes and basil, tomato flowers, dog rose fruit, and vine foliate in a florist's vase from the beginning of the twentieth century

Bouquet of blackcurrant foliage and blackberry branches, and figs in an iron pitcher (private collection)

Many colors of garden roses and blackberry branches in a terracotta deep bowl

Rose petals in an engraved crystal vase (Christian Tortu for Baccarat)

Icelandic poppies, pitahaya fruit, and poppy capsules in a glass, deep vase

Columbine seed-vessels and poppy capsules, Annabelle hydrangea, hosta leaves, and brise in a series of transparent glass carafes

Green almonds, lotus fruit, and poppy capsules in dishes covered in hosta leaves

Bouquet of dried grasses, giant reed, palm leaves, and spathiphyllum in a wood and wicker vase

Green arum lilies, tea grass, viburnum opulus, narcissus buds, and scented pelargonium leaves in two bronze vases (private collection)

Stachys lanata, bouquets of lime tree, and hosta leaves, beech tree, and angelica umbel in a hammered silver vase (private collection)

Flowering angelica branches, green hydrangea, and garlic flowers in a large zinc container (James Scott for Christian Tortu)

Country bouquet with grasses, molucella, wild carrot flower, and millet ears and flax seed-vessels

Sweet pea and lady's mantle in a silver pail (Michèle Halard)

Different color dahlias in wax vases

Poppies and smoke tree branches in a glass vase (Henry Dean)

Garden roses, capillary leaves, and hosta in a zinc vase (James Scott for Christian Tortu)

Bouquet of white lilacs, hydrangea, and viburnum opulus in an opaline glass container

Sweet pea and lily of the valley in a ceramic vase from Vallauris (private collection)

Green arum lilies, viburnum opulus, cherry tree branches, and black fritillary

Orange and black calla lilies, parrot tulips, double Uncle Tom tulips, and Lenten rose and red cestrum in a bamboo vase

Skimmia flowers, ampelopsis leaves, and pears and figs from the Barbary Coast in a painted cast-iron vase

Black pansies and purple Star clematis and sweet pea in a Nébul amethyst glass vase (Christian Tortu)

Mona Lisa anemone balls arranged in a square hand-blown glass vase

Pansies and wild asparagus in a Nébul amber-colored vase (Christian Tortu)

Garlic flower and nasturtium in a Plexiglas rectangular vase (Franco Mariotti for Christian Tortu)

Arum lilies, calla lilies, flowers, and leaves in a thin zinc vase (James Scott for Christian Tortu)

Bouquet of double white narcissus and tea grass leaves in a square hand-blown glass vase

Bianca roses arranged in glass containers

Dense bouquet of ranunculus, poppies, Toscanini roses and Oriental roses, sweet pea, viburnum opulus, and balls of ivy

Different colored nasturtium, wild strawberries, and blackberries

Round bouquet of tulips tied in raffia

Nerines and primula, and corkscrew willow

Privet berries and King Arthur orchids in a zinc square vase (James Scott for Christian Tortu)

Rose petals, blue Vanda orchids, and Lenten rose floating in silver shells (Michèle Halard)

Hydrangea, star of Bethlehem, and lentil sprouts in a deep dish filled with water

Lime tree branches, garden iris, and fritillary in long, thin vases made of stone (Christian Tortu)

Dogwood and malus branches, hawthorn fruit, and begonia leaves

Café au Lait dahlias, hydrangea and molucella

Simply violets

White hyacinth and catmint in a standing opaline pot

Cucumis, palm seed-vessels, mangosteen, and paulownia fruit

Osage orange, pears and chayote, quince, variegated eggplant, [boulestries], begonia, and [plantin] leaves in an oval terrazzo dish (Christian Tortu)

Black tacca chantieri flower, cucumis fruit, and joubarbe (a type of aeonium arboreum) placed on a pebble vase in gray terrazzo (Christian Tortu)

Red latania palm, bromeliaceae flowers, sansevieria leaves, heliconia leaves and flowers, and fern

Phaleonopsis, corkscrew willow, and helixine

Poppies and lotus fruit intertwined in kiwi liana in a white wax tube vase

Ginger flowers and green calathea, ligularia and anthurium cristallinum leaves, calla lilies, amaranth, and nasturtium in a wooden vase

Orange and green arum lilies, magnolia foliage, lotus fruit and flowering papyrus, and black and green kangaroo paws in a florist's basketwork vase.

Green anthuriums, white phalaenopsis, papyrus, and fern umbel leaves

Urns and carnivorous plant leaves (nepenthes), poppies, and columbine in an enameled stoneware vase (private collection)

Calla lilies and astrantias

White roses, astrantias, scabious fruit, and brise in a porcelain platinum vase (Christian Tortu for Raynaud-Limoges)

Sweet peas in a clear Diabolo vase (Christian Tortu)

Solanum, fern, geranium, and sweet pea in a square silvered-glass vase

Sorghum stalks and clusters of palm seed-vessels, scabious fruit and brise, and white eggplant in celadon and pale gray ceramic Empreintes vases

Anthuriums coquilles, double poppies, cotinus (smoke tree), and lacquered stones in a mismatched pair of glass vases

ACKNOWLEDGEMENTS

Sylvain and Corine's help was essential in transcribing what I have collected over so many years in my contact with nature. One was able to revive the power of the ephemeral through images and with talent and subtlety, the other was able to untangle the web of my thoughts through kindness and curiosity.

Thanks also to:

L'Alcazar
François Champsaur
La City
L'hôtel George V
Michèle and Yves Halard
L'hôtel Lancaster
Édith Mézard
Odéon-Théâtre de l'Europe
Sandrine and Reynier Pozzo di Borgo
Shozan restaurant